A 1:100,000-Scale Map of Surficial Deposits in Glacier Bay National Park and Preserve, Southeast Alaska

Natural Resource Technical Report NPS/GLBA/NRTR—2012/638

Richard A. Becker

Department of Geoscience
UW-Madison
1215 W. Dayton St.
Madison, WI 53706

Gregory P. Streveler

Icy Strait Environmental Services
P.O. Box 94
Gustavus, AK 99826

David M. Mickelson

Department of Geoscience
UW-Madison
1215 W. Dayton St.
Madison, WI 53706

October 2012

U.S. Department of the Interior
National Park Service
Natural Resource Stewardship and Science
Fort Collins, Colorado

The National Park Service, Natural Resource Stewardship and Science office in Fort Collins, Colorado publishes a range of reports that address natural resource topics of interest and applicability to a broad audience in the National Park Service and others in natural resource management, including scientists, conservation and environmental constituencies, and the public.

The Natural Resource Technical Report Series is used to disseminate results of scientific studies in the physical, biological, and social sciences for both the advancement of science and the achievement of the National Park Service mission. The series provides contributors with a forum for displaying comprehensive data that are often deleted from journals because of page limitations.

All manuscripts in the series receive the appropriate level of peer review to ensure that the information is scientifically credible, technically accurate, appropriately written for the intended audience, and designed and published in a professional manner. This document and its accompanying map received formal peer review by six scientists with expertise in Glacier Bay's surficial geology: E. Cowan, R. Goodwin, G. Larson, G. McKenzie, R. Motyka, and G. Wiles. Some of these scientists looked at this document multiple times during its development. None of these scientists were involved with the collection, analysis, or reporting of the data.

Views, statements, findings, conclusions, recommendations, and data in this report do not necessarily reflect views and policies of the National Park Service, U.S. Department of the Interior. Mention of trade names or commercial products does not constitute endorsement or recommendation for use by the U.S. Government.

This report is available from the Natural Resource Publications Management website (http://www.nature.nps.gov/publications/nrpm/).

Please cite this publication as:

Becker, R. A., G. P. Streveler, and D. M. Mickelson. 2012. A 1:100,000-scale map of surficial deposits in Glacier Bay National Park and Preserve, Southeast Alaska. Natural Resource Technical Report NPS/GLBA/NRTR—2012/638. National Park Service, Fort Collins, Colorado.

NPS 1321/117432, October 2012

Contents

iii

Contents (continued)

Figures

Tables

Appendices

Abstract

A 1:100,000-scale surficial geology map of Glacier Bay National Park and Preserve was produced by digitizing published maps, interpreting aerial photography, and systematizing personal observations. The map area also includes the Icy Strait islands, Gustavus, and the Canadian portion of the Bay's watershed. Mapping efforts were concentrated on the lowlands, as these deposits are most abundant, complex, and relevant to visitors and management. The 1948 set of aerial photographs was primarily used in mapping, as that set provides the most complete coverage of the map area with the least amount of vegetation, but older and younger photos were also consulted. Sediments were classified in terms of age (Pleistocene, Holocene, or currently active) and how they were deposited (*i.e.*, by streams, glaciers, wind, gravity, *etc.*). In places where there was some knowledge of underlying sediments, this information was captured as well. The result is a map that covers 2475 km^2 (exclusive of areas covered by water, ice, or without mappable sediments) and has 1364 "polygons" belonging to 17 different sediment types.

Acknowledgments

The authors with to sincerely thank the following people for their help with this project: B. Eichenlaub provided us with numerous GIS files, including digitized aerial photography covering the entire park and preserve. J. Kington lent technical GIS assistance and a consistent willingness to set aside what he was working on to answer a question. R. Yerxa made the park's aerial photography collection and conference room available. L. Sharman facilitated the collaboration and provided an enjoyable day in the field. B. Heise and his colleagues at the National Park Service's Geologic Resources Division (GRD) took an interest in the project and marshaled the financial resources to enable it to take flight: substantial funding was provided by the GRD with additional funding provided by the NPS Inventory and Monitoring Program at the national and Southeast Alaska Network levels. Lastly we wish to acknowledge our reviewers: E. Cowan, R. Goodwin, G. Larson, G. McKenzie, R. Motyka, and G. Wiles gave thoughtful reviews that substantially improved the map and this companion to it. The authors claim responsibility for any shortcomings that remain.

Introduction

The geologic story of the park consists of two distinct chapters: one recorded in the bedrock, which ranges from 400 to 7 million years in age, and a second much younger story written in the surficial sediments whose ages with few exceptions range from *ca.* 20,000 years ago to the present. Much attention has been devoted to both of these topics, but published maps are almost entirely restricted to the bedrock geology (*e.g.*, Rossman, 1958; MacKevett *et al.*, 1971; Gehrels and Berg, 1992; Brew and Plafker, in prep). None of the surficial sediment maps are park-wide, being limited to only a few areas instead (*e.g.*, McKenzie, 1970; Mickelson, 1971). Until now there has been no consolidated source of information on the surficial deposits, despite their great importance as a repository of landscape history in a park renowned for its environmental dynamism (*e.g.*, Cooper, 1937). Furthermore, the surficial deposits host most of the lowland plant communities and are an important influence on them, a topic of special interest in Glacier Bay. Lastly, the surficial deposits serve as the sole aquifer for Gustavus, the park's gateway community.

The purpose of this project is to compile a 1:100,000-scale surficial geology map of Glacier Bay National Park and Preserve. At the Park Service's request, we have supplemented the published literature with our own observations, gained formally and informally over the years, and made reasonable suppositions based on both sources of knowledge. This summary represents what is known, or is likely to be true, about the map area's surficial units. The uncertainty level varies from Muir Inlet's relatively well-studied deposits, through the moderately well-known and accessible deposits within the park's Neoglacial ice limits, to the more conjectural map units in the largely unstudied and thickly vegetated areas outside those limits.

The intended audience includes park managers, other researchers from an array of scientific disciplines, park interpretive and educational staff, and members of the general public that are particularly interested in the origins of landscapes. As a result, this text attempts to use a language that is accessible to non-geologists while preserving the technical information desired by specialists.

Study Area

Glacier Bay National Park and Preserve, and some adjacent areas (the Icy Strait / Cross Sound islands, Gustavus, and the Canadian portion of the Bay's watershed), were mapped (Fig. 1). Emphasis was placed on the deposits of the "lowlands;" less attention was given to high-altitude areas as deposits there are generally thin or absent. No attempt was made to map deposits below mean high tide, although there is a growing body of literature on the area's submarine sedimentary geology (*e.g.*, Cowan *et al.*, 1988; Seramur *et al.*, 1997; Cowan *et al.*, 2010; Trusel *et al.*, 2010). We use the term "lowlands" to refer to areas with gentle to moderate slopes. These areas are generally within a few hundred meters of sea level, but in places where moderate slopes are fairly continuous, such as around Hugh Miller Inlet and Scidmore Bay, the actual elevations may climb higher than 600 m and include rounded ridge tops. In other locations, such as along Rendu Inlet, which is steep-sided, the lowlands are limited to elevations of less than 30 m by our definition. Our procedure was to start mapping at sea level and work up slope until mappable deposits became discontinuous; as indicated above, that elevation was quite variable.

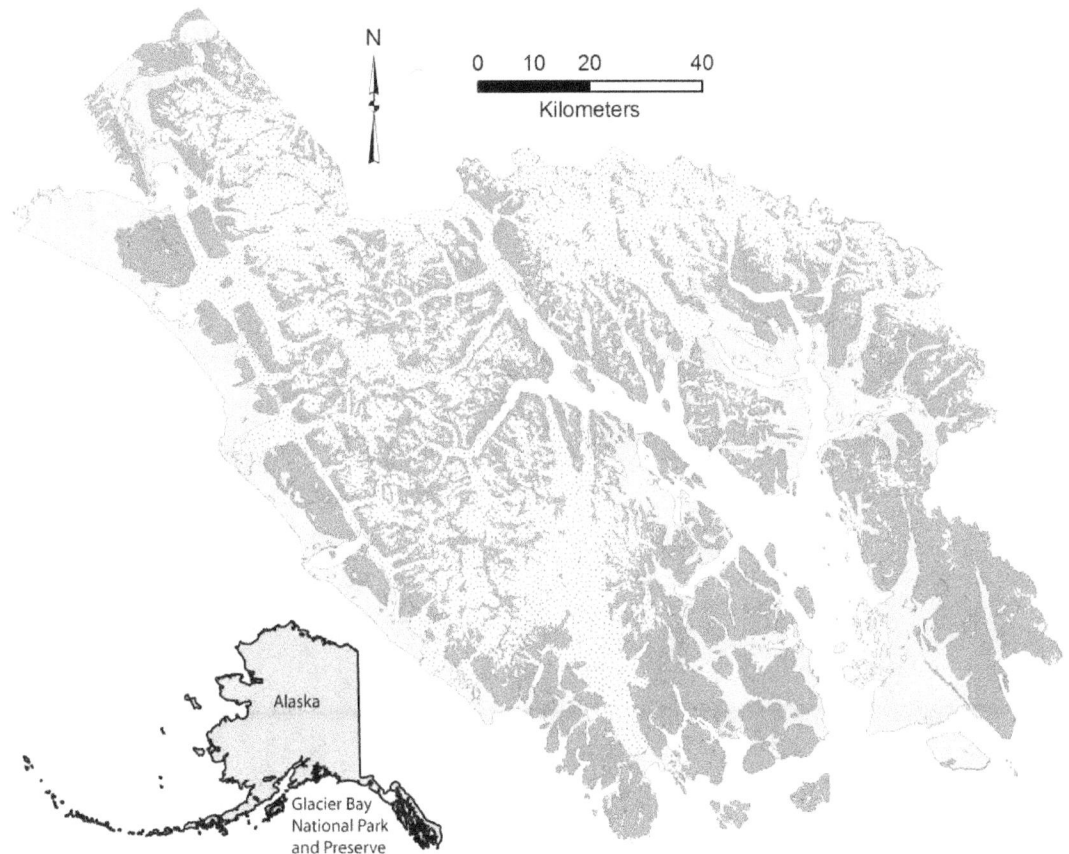

Figure 1: Glacier Bay National Park is located at the northern end of southeastern Alaska. The mapped area includes the National Park and Preserve, the Cross Sound / Icy Strait islands, and the Canadian portion of the Bay's watershed. Emphasis was placed on the lowlands; less attention was given to mountainous areas and no attempt was made to map deposits below the mean high tide line. Above, yellow areas represent sediments, gray areas represent places where there are no mappable sediments, and the white unit with blue speckles denotes areas of snow / ice. See the methods section for details on how these categories were defined.

Methods

Defining the Map Units

Map Unit Minimum Requirements
A sedimentary unit was considered mappable if:
1) Sediments were estimated to be generally greater than 2 m thick, and
2) They comprise a more or less contiguous unit larger than 30,000 m^2 (which is ~ 5½ US football fields, including the end zones).

In almost every case we could only estimate sediment thicknesses based on aerial photograph interpretation and our experiences in this landscape.

Sediment Bodies
These map units are based on the dominant sediment type listed below and its inferred age. The sediment types are as follows:

Stream Sediment (S) –layered sand and/or gravel with rounded particles deposited by streams. This sediment type includes outwash, alluvial fan, and delta sediments deposited above lake or sea level (*i.e.*, the topset beds). See figures B1 through B4, B12, B17, B18, B20 through B22, and B26 in the photo appendix for examples.

Ice-Contact Sediment Complex (I) – a mixture of rounded-to-angular sediments of all sizes with varying degrees of layering that were deposited on, adjacent to, or under glacial ice. Includes eskers, kames, hummocky topography, and undifferentiated collapse features. See figures B2 and B7 through B13 in the photo appendix for examples.

Till (T) – rounded-to-angular sediment of any size directly deposited by a glacier and not inferred to overlie other thick deposits. See figures B5, B6, B12 through B15, B17 through B19, and B25 in the photo appendix for examples.

Till Over Layered Sediment (T/S) – till lying upon layered sediment, such as stream or lake deposits. See figures B4, B19, and B20 in the photo appendix, as well as the photos for till and the various kinds of layered sediment.

Lake Sediment Complex (L) – layered sediment, generally sand, silt and/or clay in particle size, which was deposited below the surface of a lake. Includes lake floors and the underwater portions of deltas and beaches. See figures B14 through B16 in the photo appendix for examples.

Marine Sediment Complex (M) – deposits of rounded particles ranging in size from clay to boulders that are usually layered and were formed by marine processes. In many cases, because we did not map below the mean high tide, these deposits have been lifted above sea level by isostatic rebound. See figures B21 and B26 in the photo appendix for examples.

Colluvium (C) – loose, unsorted deposits at the foot of a slope or cliff, brought there by gravity. See figures B1, B3, B11, and B22 in the photo appendix for examples.

Wind-Blown Sediment (W) – sand deposited by the wind. We did not map loess, which is silt deposited by the wind, because nowhere in the map area is it 2 m thick.

Map units, except for colluvium, were also classified based on the known or inferred age of the surface, or (when a significant stratigraphy was known) the age of the uppermost deposit more than 2 m thick. The age classification is as follows:

1- Modern   - deposits less than about 100 calendar years old
2- Holocene   - deposits between about 100 calendar and 10,000 ^{14}C years old
3- Pleistocene   - deposits more than about 10,000 ^{14}C years old

The distinction between Modern and Holocene was often difficult to make because of the rapid changes in vegetation that take place on recently stabilized surfaces.

Combining these two classification schemes results in the following map unit designations:

1. MODERN
- Stream Sediment (S1) – deposits that show evidence of recent stream activity; vegetation absent to shrubby. See figures B1 through B3, B17, and B22 in the photo appendix.
- Ice-Contact Sediment Complex (I1) – sediment interpreted to be lying on top of ice that is actively melting and causing the sediment to collapse. See figures B2 and B7 through B12 in the photo appendix.
- Till (T1) – till surfaces still in contact with glacial ice or obviously of very recent origin. See figures B5, B6, and B13.
- Lake Sediment Complex (L1) - the sediments of actively lowering or recently drained glacial lakes. This unit is common in the Brady and Muir provinces. See figures B15 and B16.
- Marine Sediment Complex (M1) – includes active outer coast beaches and the currently active portions of isostatically rebounding beaches in the southeastern and western portions of the park. Because we only mapped deposits above mean high tide level, M1 includes only upper beach features, unlike the M2 and M3 classifications, which include sediments deposited in deep water as well as beach deposits. See figure B21.
- Wind-Blown Sediment (W1) - Used sparingly for sand dunes and sand barrens at Dry Bay, Gustavus, and Strawberry Island.

2. HOLOCENE
- Stream Sediment (S2) - deposits that have not been active recently (*i.e.*, if inactive on the aerial photographs that we were examining, which were typically, although certainly not always, from 1948. Some aerial photos were as new as the mid-1990s.) See figures B17, B20, and B21.
- Ice-Contact Sediment Complex (I2) – substantially inactive collapse topography, associated with formerly stagnant ice bodies. See figure B18.
- Till (T2) – till surfaces not in direct contact with ice and not of very recent origin; not known to overlie layered sediments. In certain cases, especially in Muir Inlet, some till surfaces younger than 100 calendar years were mapped as T2 because they had become stabilized and thoroughly covered with vegetation. See figures B17 through B19.
- Till Over Layered Sediment (T/S2) – till surfaces not in direct contact with glacier ice, not of very recent origin, and overlying thick deposits of layered sediments. The buried layered sediments are typically outwash, but in places are known to be lake sediments instead. See figures B19 and B20.

- <u>Lake Sediment Complex</u> (L2) – the sediments of former lakes related to Neoglacial ice margins. Also used for the marshes northwest of Lituya Bay, which are interpreted to represent filled in lakes and are separated from the sea by beach ridges. See figure B16.
- <u>Marine Sediment Complex</u> (M2) – Uplifted intertidal and sub-tidal sediments including beaches as well as other marine sediments. See figure B21.

3. PLEISTOCENE

   Certain areas outside the Neoglacial ice limits appear to contain extensive Pleistocene deposits. We identified such deposits on Excursion Ridge, Pleasant Island and around Dundas Bay based on: 1) scattered outcrops visited by the authors over the years, 2) lowlands at elevations known to have been below sea level at the end of the Pleistocene (Mann and Streveler, 2008). We did not map them as present along the park's southwestern shores, because these surfaces generally appear wave-washed and we interpret that the sediments fail to obtain the minimum thicknesses of 2 m. Pleistocene deposits are also mapped on the terraces flanking Lituya Bay based on our own personal observations and those of Mann (1983).

- <u>Stream Sediment</u> (S3) – sediment in the Lituya Bay area outside the Neoglacial ice limit as mapped by Mann (1983).
- <u>Ice-Contact Sediment Complex</u> (I3) – ice-contact sand and gravel near Pt. Carolus.
- <u>Till</u> (T3) – till outside the Neoglacial ice limit in the Lituya Bay area, largely as inferred from clusters of moraines identified by Mann (1983). See figure B25.
- <u>Marine Sediment Complex</u> (M3) - Uplifted intertidal and sub-tidal sediments including beaches as well as other marine sediments. Mapped on low elevation, low-relief surfaces, on which marine deposits are known to exist (Falls Creek, Pleasant Island), or are considered likely (Dundas, outer coast benches). This category also likely includes extensive glacial and stream deposits as well as bedrock surfaces, but we cannot easily distinguish these differences from aerial photos. See figure B26.

The sediment bodies that we have mapped are thus classified both in terms of their antiquity and their sedimentary composition, with one exception: *we did not subdivide the colluvium category by age*. This was primarily because these deposits have generally formed slowly over long periods of time, but also because they commonly lack datable materials. We are unaware of any dates on colluvium deposits anywhere in the map area. In any event, colluvium is a minor constituent of Glacier Bay's surficial geology, covering less than 0.5% of the map area.

Glaciers
Glaciers are mapped as they occurred in *ca.* 2000. They were derived from SRTM (Shuttle Radar Topography Mission) elevation data and a mosaic of high-quality LandSat images produced by NASA. The images in the LandSat mosaic were acquired between August 1, 1999 and September 3, 2002 (MDA Federal, 2004). The lack of discontinuities in the mosaic's snow cover suggests that all of the images that comprise it are from late summer and thus are appropriate for inferring the extent of glaciers and perennial snow patches. The SRTM data were acquired by the Space Shuttle *Endeavour* in February 2000 (Farr *et al.*, 2007).

The mapping of glaciers was largely automated; this is the only map unit that was created with the assistance of an algorithm. The raster calculator of ESRI's ArcGIS 9.2 was used to identify pixels in the LandSat mosaic that had a color consistent with snow or ice (Appendix C has a detailed explanation of our methods). This rapidly and correctly identified most areas, but failed to select regions covered by thin clouds, supraglacial debris, or dark shadows. In addition, some areas of shallow water were incorrectly selected. These nearshore selections were small and isolated, so they were removed by filtering the results by size. Portions of glaciers obscured by clouds, debris, or shadows were manually digitized using the SRTM elevation data as a guide. This manual effort was concentrated along glacier termini because it was here that the automated approached struggled the most (the majority of the glaciers in the map area are in retreat and are thus covered with debris in their lower-elevation reaches) and because it is here that the glaciers are in direct contact with the primary target of this mapping project, the unconsolidated sediments.

The result is that the confidence level in the accuracy of glacier extents varies as a function of elevation and slope. In the flat and low-elevation valley bottoms, such as along the fronts of the Casement, Carroll, and Brady Glaciers, we have a high degree of confidence in the accuracy of the glacier extents. In higher elevation areas, and on moderate-to-steep slopes, we have a low degree of confidence. Rather, in these places, the mapped extents should be interpreted more as a reasonable suggestion, based on the consistent application of a generally valid algorithm. There are likely consistent differences between north-facing and south-facing slopes due to shading and, in any event, it is challenging in snow-covered areas to determine whether the snow lies directly upon the bedrock (in which case it should *not* be mapped as part of a glacier) or upon glacier ice (in which case it should be). For that reason, the glacier map unit is labeled as "snow / ice" as that is more accurately what it is. Readers interested in documenting the changes in glacial extents are discouraged from using this map as a reference and are referred to primary sources such as photographs and satellite imagery instead.

Water Bodies
The National Park Service provided us with a GIS file containing lake extents. We modified these extents in a few places on the basis of the SRTM elevation data, but in general, little was changed. The marine shoreline was mapped from the SRTM data.

Areas of "No Mappable Sediments"
Areas not mapped as water, snow/ice, or some kind of sediment are classified as having "no mappable sediments." This map unit might simply be called "bedrock," but we prefer the term "no mappable sediments" because it better captures reality. In many locations these are areas of thin, patchy till or colluvium interspersed with bare bedrock outcrops. No mappable sediments best captures this unit's essence. In addition to its gray unit color, it is identified on the map by the letter "N" in potentially confusing locations. See figures B1, B3, B12, B19, B23, and B24 for examples of this unit.

Applying the Map Units
Much literature exists on the surficial sediment in the park, due in large part to the sequence of excellent studies in the Muir Inlet area by the Institute of Polar Studies (IPS) at The Ohio State University (*e.g.*, Price, 1964; Goldthwait, 1966; Haselton, 1966; McKenzie, 1970; Mickelson, 1971; Goodwin, 1984; Anderson *et al.*, 1986). Published or otherwise reported information for the remainder of the park is sparse. Consequently, we took somewhat different approaches for the Muir Inlet area and the remaining portion of the map area.

Mapping Procedures – non-Muir Inlet Areas

The entire map, with the exception of the Muir Inlet area, was first drafted by Streveler at park headquarters; here he had access to aerial photographs and the park's library. Several publications were useful as general background, but only a few actually provided maps and even fewer of those were comprehensive. Consequently, the first draft of these poorly mapped areas was created by photo interpretation, using Streveler's history of observation as a guide where possible. Aerial photographs from 1929, 1948, and 1996, supplemented with satellite imagery, were used. The mapping was aided by topographic maps generated from the SRTM data as a base.

Mapping Procedures – Adams Inlet

Adams Inlet was treated separately from the rest of Muir Inlet because of the excellent and detailed surficial mapping that was done there by Garry McKenzie (1970). McKenzie used a 1:63,360 Juneau D-6 quadrangle as a base and was assisted by aerial photography and detailed field work, measuring 97 stratigraphic sections over the course of two field seasons. Becker digitized McKenzie's map and converted his units into the ones used here based on the unit descriptions given in McKenzie (1970). The conversion is given in Table 1:

McKenzie's Classification	Our Classification
Seal River Formation	Stream Sediment 2
Glacier Bay Formation:	
Glaciolacustrine member	Lake Sediment Complex 2
Ice-contact stratified drift	Ice-Contact Sediment Complex 2
Ground and ablation moraine	Till 2
Berg Formation	Stream Sediment 2
Adams Formation	Lake Sediment Complex 2
Van Horn Formation:	
Lower gravel member	Stream Sediment 2
Forest Creek Formation	Marine Sediment Complex 3
Granite Canyon Till	Till 3

Table 1. The conversion of McKenzie's (1970) map units into the ones used in this report. Because McKenzie spent two summers in the field, mapping the deposits of a much smaller area, he was able to give names to each individual layer; we are forced to generalize.

This conversion results in a less detailed map than McKenzie's original. For example, the Seal River Formation, the Berg Formation, and the Van Horn's lower gravel member all equate to Stream Sediment 2 within our classification scheme. This loss of detail is unfortunate, but it is required if there are to be consistent map units across our entire map area. Readers interested in Adams Inlet in particular are referred to McKenzie (1970).

Mapping Procedures - The Rest of Muir Inlet

The remainder of Muir Inlet was mapped in Madison, Wisconsin by Mickelson using 1996 black and white Digital Orthophoto Quarter Quadrangles (DOQQs) using the same criteria as Streveler. A DOQQ is a high-resolution aerial photograph that covers a quarter of a quadrangle and has been modified to remove the distortion created by the topography. This enables DOQQs to be used as maps. These were supplemented by other aerial photographs and topographic maps.

We used the extensive literature on Muir Inlet as a guide to our mapping. Goodwin (1984) described deposits in Muir Inlet's southern part. Haselton (1966) showed deposits west of Muir Inlet on several maps and described stratigraphic sections on both sides of Muir Inlet. Price (1964) mapped landforms in front of the Casement Glacier. This was large-scale mapping of individual eskers and other landforms, so that map was generalized considerably for this 1:100,000-scale map. Mickelson (1971) and Syverson (1992) mapped areas around the Burroughs Glacier and along Wachusett Inlet and these maps were generalized as well. All of these areas were mapped onto the DOQQs.

Producing the Final Map

Becker digitized published maps, Streveler's and Mickelson's mapping, delimited modern glacier and water extents, and then merged all of this information into a single digital layer using ArcGIS 9.2. While digitizing the authors' mapping, he checked for inaccuracies and inconsistencies and identified them to Streveler and Mickelson for clarification. Once the digital files were assembled, the authors repeatedly proofed them against their original mapping until all observed errors were corrected.

Results

The result of this effort to compile and systematize published and unpublished information on the surficial sediments of Glacier Bay National Park and Preserve, and a few adjacent areas, is a map covering 15,932 km^2 with 3624 different "polygons" belonging to 21 map units. Excluding areas of water, snow / ice, and no mappable sediments leaves 2475 km^2 (16% of the total map area) that is sediment covered by our definition. The most abundant units are Holocene Till (T2), Holocene Stream Sediment (S2), and Modern Stream Sediment (S1). Collectively, Holocene-aged sediments cover 70% of the map area while Modern and Pleistocene sediments cover 19% and 11%, respectively. Additional details are in Tables 2 and 3.

Classification	% of Map Area	Area (km^2)
Water	24	3835
Snow / Ice	31	4907
Surficial Sediments	16	2474
No Mappable Sediments	29	4673

Table 2. The relative frequency of water, snow / ice, and surficial sediments in Glacier Bay.

	Stream Sediments	Ice-Contact Sediments	Till	Till/Layered Sediments	Lake Sediments	Marine Sediments	Wind-Blown Sediments	Colluvium	Total:
Modern	13%	2%	1%	x	~0%	3%	~0%	~0%	19%
Holocene	26%	6%	27%	8%	1%	2%	x	x	70%
Pleistocene	~0%	~0%	5%	x	x	5%	x	x	11%
Total:	39%	8%	33%	8%	2%	10%	~0%	~0%	100%

Table 3. The relative frequency of map units as a percentage of the total *sediment-covered* area. The units are defined in the methods section. Categories, such as "Modern Till over Layered Sediments" and "Pleistocene Lake Sediments," which are not present in the map area, are marked with an "x." All three age categories of "Colluvium" are blank because this unit was not subdivided by age, an undifferentiated value of ~0% is reported in the totals section. Totals might differ from expected values due to rounding; all values are correct to the nearest one's position. A tilde is used to emphasize this for values that were rounded down to zero; unlike the units marked with an "x," there are in fact units of this classification on the map.

12

Discussion of Sedimentary Provinces

To facilitate discussion of regional sedimentary characteristics, we have divided the map area into eight provinces (Fig. 2). Province boundaries delineate areas with distinctive sedimentary characteristics. Certain of them contain prominent sedimentary deposits which have already received formation names in the literature. In those instances we adhere to these names. In the case of unnamed deposits we simply describe their nature.

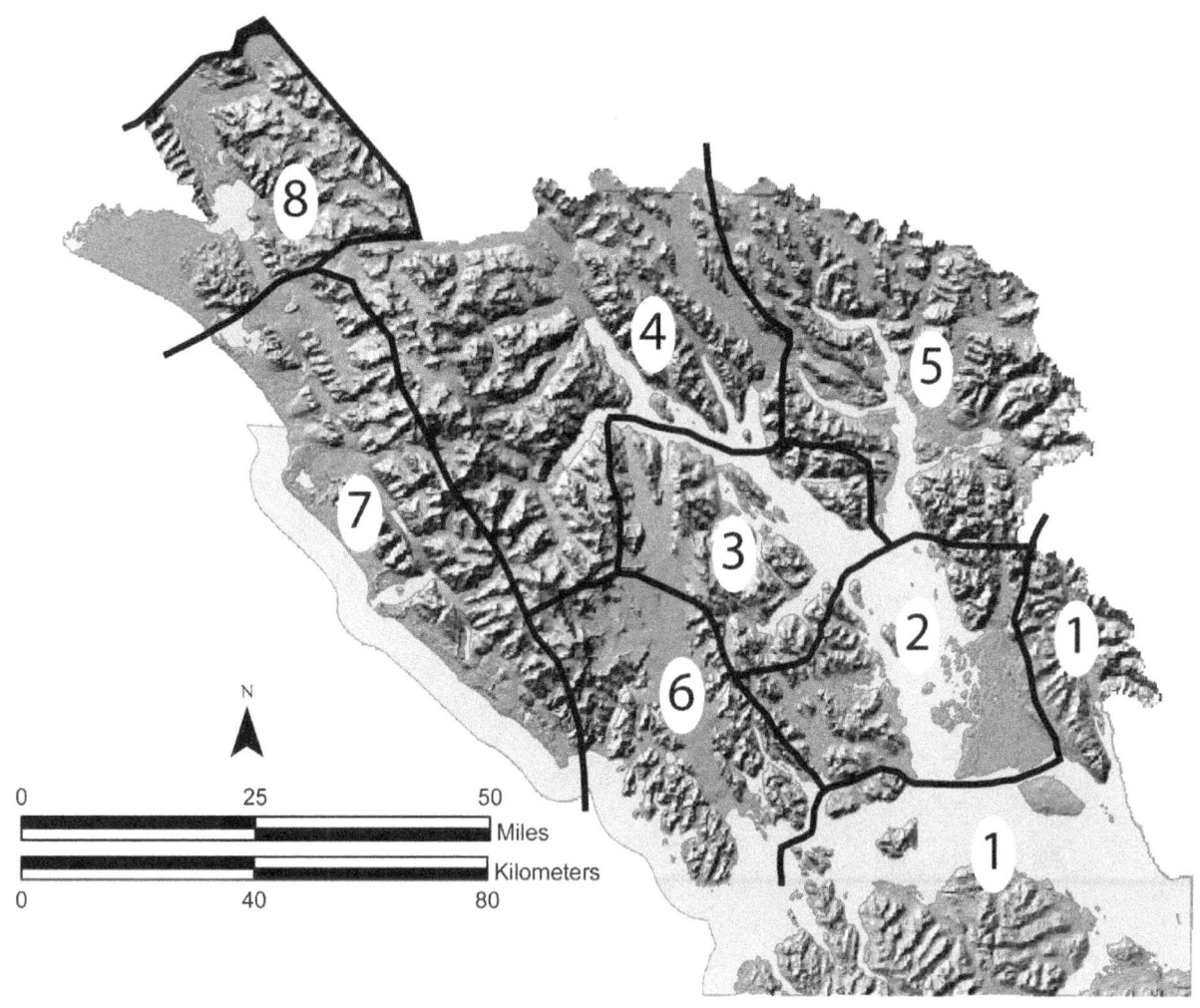

Figure 2: The eight sedimentary provinces that we use to facilitate a discussion of the characteristic sediments and history of the map area's different regions.

1- Excursion (p. 14)
2- Lower Bay (p.15)
3- Mid Bay (p. 16)

4- Upper Bay (p. 17)
5- Muir (p. 18)
6- Brady (p. 20)

7- Lituya (p. 21)
8- Alsek (p. 22)

The Excursion Province

Characterization
The Excursion River watershed is the largest in the map area that was not directly impacted by Neoglacial ice. Its valley floor contains extensive Holocene stream sediment (S2) and is probably underlain by Pleistocene glaciomarine deposits (M3, but not shown on the map because they are buried by S2). Pleistocene ice flowing westward across Excursion Ridge left thick glacial deposits (T3) on the ridge's west side. Uplifted Pleistocene glaciomarine deposits (M3) appear to be extensive on the lowlands east of Dundas Bay, and Pleasant Island. Other Icy Strait islands are free of extensive sedimentary deposits.

Significant Sedimentary Records
An extensive but almost unstudied late Pleistocene record exists in the glacial and glacier-related deposits throughout the southern portions of the Excursion province. They are well exposed in the Falls Creek area of Excursion Ridge. These deposits include thick till (T3), ice-contact sediments (I3), delta and uplifted marine components (M3). A former beach now about 60 m above present high tide was dated to 13,900 ^{14}C yr BP (Mann and Streveler, 2008).

Information Sources
Map units were drawn based on the examination of aerial photography, guided by existing literature and personal observation. The most complete on-the-ground information for this province comes from detailed observation during development of the Falls Creek hydropower project (Mann and Streveler, 2008), but many observations of beach and creek exposures have been made by Streveler over the years throughout the province.

The Lower-Bay Province

Characterization
Remnants of an immense late Neoglacial outwash plain (S2) now fringe lower Glacier Bay, and remain as islands within the bay. Overriding ice in a final advance to Icy Strait about 250 calendar years ago dissected and deformed portions of that plain; undisturbed outer fringes remain northeast of Point Carolus and especially in the Gustavus forelands. Large morainal complexes are built into the lower Beartrack River valley, trapping a former glacial lake. They extend southward to Points Gustavus and Carolus. A second large Neoglacial outwash plain (S2) was built into the Dundas River valley from several ice sources to the north and east. It has been partially reworked by modern outwash (S1) from the Dundas River. The high rates of isostatic rebound (~25 mm/yr) (Larsen *et al.*, 2004; Motyka *et al.*, 2007) and the relatively flat terrain have combined to produce notable areas of raised marine sediments in this province.

Significant Sedimentary Records

Beardslee Formation
Abbreviated from Connor *et al.* (2009), this formation includes the Beardslee Islands, the perimeter of Beartrack Cove, the Gustavus forelands, Lars and Netland Islands on the Bay's western shore near Berg Bay, and discontinuous pockets along island and mainland shores in the mid-bay. Sediments are composed of deformed and eroded river (S2), lake (L2), and marine sediments (M2), in some localities sparsely overlain by till (T/S2) or wind-deposited sands and silts (W1). Water-lain deposits rarely consist of particle sizes larger than fine gravel except in the formation's northern extent. Silt and sand crop out along many shores. A late Neoglacial lateral moraine cuts NE-SW across the Beardslee Formation. Outside the moraine, the Gustavus forelands are unmodified by ice.

The large outwash complex (S2) veneering Dundas Valley appears to have been constructed from five distributaries of late Neoglacial Glacier Bay ice, assisted to a minor degree by Brady Glacier ice. Exposed vertical sections exist along the valley's rivers, but remain unstudied. The valley has not been overridden by Neoglacial ice, but has been modified at the Dundas River mouth by isostatic rebound and ongoing beach processes. Its western margin is also currently being modified by the Dundas River.

Information Sources
Lower Glacier Bay has been described by Connor *et al.* (2009), who summarize a long experience of observations there. The Dundas River valley has been studied only at its mouth (Mann and Streveler, 2008).

The Mid-Bay Province

Characterization
All lowlands in the area from Geikie Inlet to Reid Inlet were overridden by Neoglacial ice. In much of the area the bedrock was scoured, leaving only pockets of till (N). In the area centering on Hugh Miller Inlet, however, thick till (T2) covers many of the ridges. Valley heads appear to have functioned as cul-de-sacs, where ice from the Brady and Glacier Bay systems tended to meet, stagnate, and leave thick, complex deposits.

Significant Sedimentary Records
Thick deposits have accumulated at the head of Geikie Inlet, Weird Bay, near Scidmore Glacier, and at the head of Charpentier Inlet. Though almost completely unstudied, they appear to document a complex Holocene history of ice stagnation, outwash accumulation (S2) and ice-dammed lake formation (L2).

Small areas of sediment accumulation along Reid Inlet and lower Ptarmigan Creek include early Holocene till (T2) and uplifted marine silt (M2), as well as organic matter in and between glacial deposits (T2) that document a series of ice advances and retreats.

Information Sources
Information on this area was gathered from Goldthwait (1961), Connor *et al.* (2009), Lawson (*ca*. 2009), and observation over the years by the authors. Wiles *et al.* (2011) documented Holocene ice advances in the mid-bay region using dendrochronology.

The Upper-Bay Province

Characterization
In this scoured and recently deglaciated northern end of Glacier Bay, mappable sediments are generally restricted to pockets and veneers of till (T2 or N, depending on thickness and area), colluvium (C), and (along eastern Tarr Inlet) stratified terraces that have the appearance of being ice-contact sediments (I2).

Significant Sedimentary Records
There is a highly visible pocket of lake sediment (L2) about halfway up Tarr Inlet's northeast side where the Grand Pacific Glacier dammed a partially deglaciated tributary valley about 100 calendar years ago. This lake sediment, however, does not meet our minimum area threshold rule, so it is not mapped.

Information Sources
Mapping of this area was based on Haselton (1984) and observations over the years by the authors. Brief studies of these deposits have produced no datable materials. Wood was found incorporated in glacial sediments near Vivid Lake but it has not been dated.

The Muir Province

Characterization

Muir Inlet was extensively glaciated during the late Pleistocene. Till from that episode (T3) has been recognized along Muir Inlet and its tributaries. This till is only exposed in outcrop and therefore is not mapped. Pleistocene deposits were mostly eroded from higher areas by Neoglacial ice. Characteristic of this province is the extensive and thick accumulation of Holocene lake (L2) and outwash sediments (S2) throughout the lowlands.

Unlike the Upper Bay, which may have contained ice through much of the time between the retreat of Pleistocene ice (*ca.* 11,000 ^{14}C yrs ago) and the early advance of Neoglacial ice several thousand years later, most of Muir, Adams, and Wachusett Inlets were substantially deglaciated. Glaciers on higher land surrounding the inlets produced huge amounts of outwash (S2) that apparently filled the inlets to well above present sea level (Goldthwait, 1986). This gravel wedge grew southward, but then was apparently dammed by ice filling the West Arm, blocking the mid-Bay area and repeatedly producing a large lake into which fine-grained sediment was deposited (L2) (Goodwin, 1984). As the ice continued to advance down Muir Inlet, outwash was deposited on top of the lake sediment in many places. This ice advance scoured, but did not completely remove, these sediments, which now form bluffs along the shore. Nearly all of these mid-to-late Holocene deposits have a cover of Neoglacial till (T/S2). A representative stratigraphy from Muir Inlet is shown (Fig. 3).

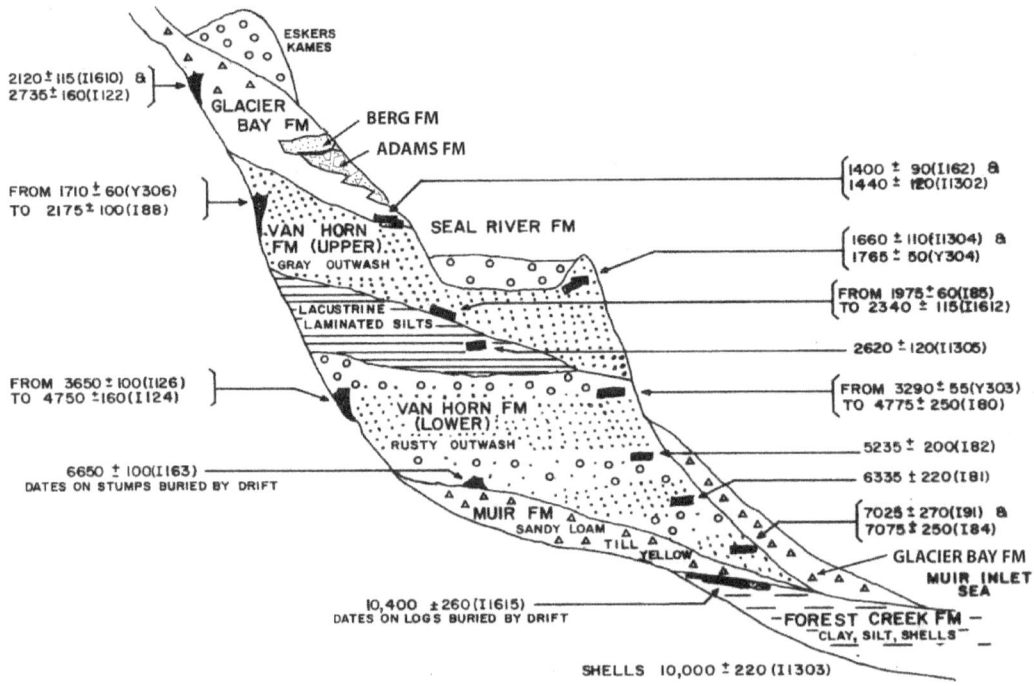

Figure 3: Muir Inlet area's generalized stratigraphy. Compiled from many outcrops by many researchers, we modified it from Goldthwait (1986) and Goodwin (1984). Radiocarbon years BP are shown with one standard deviation, indicating that there is a 66% chance that the true age falls within that range. Many more wood samples have been dated since this was compiled in the mid-1980s (Lawson, 2011).

18

Significant Sedimentary Records

Muir Inlet and its tributaries contain thick deposits that retain records of the late Pleistocene glaciation and much of the Holocene (Fig. 3). There is late Pleistocene till (T3) exposed at the base of a few of the outcrops in this province (such as the Muir Formation of Haselton (1966) and McKenzie's (1970) Granite Canyon till). The next youngest unit is the Forest Creek Formation (M3), which is composed of shell-bearing clay and silt (Haselton, 1966). Above this unit is the Van Horn Formation, consisting of a lower gravel unit (S2), a middle silt unit (L2), and an upper sandy, gravelly unit (S2) (Haselton, 1966). It is widespread in the Muir Inlet area. This unit once filled all of Muir Inlet and its tributaries creating a valley floor well above present sea level (Goldthwait, 1961; McKenzie, 1986). Deposition of the upper Van Horn Formation (S2) and advancing West Arm ice dammed lakes in the lower Muir Inlet area at times between 2,500 to 1,200 ^{14}C yrs BP (Goodwin, 1984). The lake sediment of the Adams Formation (L2) and the stream sediment of the Berg Formation (S2) were deposited as Neoglacial ice advanced across the area, ultimately exterminating the lakes (McKenzie, 1970).

Most of the area is capped by Neoglacial till (T2, or T/S2, if thought to be overlying layered sediments (stream and/or lake deposits) that are ≥2 m in thickness) and related deposits of the Glacier Bay Formation (I2 and L2) (Haselton, 1966). Outwash deposited by retreating late Neoglacial ice was called the Seal River Formation (S2) in Adams Inlet (McKenzie, 1970), but that outwash was considered part of the Glacier Bay Formation (S2) in Wachusett Inlet (Mickelson, 1971).

Information Sources

From the 1950s to the 1990s, students of R. P. Goldthwait ("Doc G") at The Ohio State University conducted research projects on the glacial history and genesis of glacial deposits in Muir, Wachusett, and Adams Inlets. See for example Goldthwait (1961; 1966) and Anderson *et al.* (1986). Some studies, like those of Peterson and McKenzie (1968), Taylor (1962), and Larson (1978) were strictly glaciology. The reports that include information about the deposits include Price (1964), McKenzie (1970), Haselton (1966), Mickelson (1971), Goodwin (1984), and papers by these individuals in Anderson *et al.* (1986). Ross Powell, another student of Goldthwait, along with his collaborators, has extensively studied the submarine record in Muir Inlet and elsewhere (Powell, 1983; Powell and Carlson, 1997).

The Brady Province

Characterization

Early Neoglacial advances of the Brady Glacier have built complex assemblages of glacial (T2), outwash (S2) and lake deposits (L2) into the Taylor and Dundas Bay lowlands, as well as into the small fjords from Palma Bay to Graves Harbor. Remnants of Pleistocene deposits are found outside the Neoglacial limits. Unlike Glacier Bay ice, that of the Brady has remained in contact with its late Neoglacial features, and so many sedimentary processes remain active today.

Significant Sedimentary Records

An early Neoglacial outwash/morainal complex (S2 and T2) has been exposed by river erosion along the upper Dixon River where it abuts the end of Boussole Valley. Extensive deposits formed by the Brady Glacier's early Neoglacial advance are found in most valleys around the glacier's lower reaches, but are not well exposed.

Information Sources

The Dixon Harbor Biological Survey provided Streveler with considerable opportunity to view sedimentary features in the western half of the province and it provided Derksen (1976) with the opportunity to intensively study the entire area. Derksen's reconnaissance mapping has guided our mapping, but as is the case for other provinces, we have relied on aerial photo interpretation to provide most details. Detailed information on the advance of the Brady Glacier to its latest Neoglacial maximum has been recently provided by Capps *et al.* (2011).

The Lituya Province

Characterization
This province's sedimentary history has been dominated by Desolation Valley, which has collected ice from the Fairweather Range and shunted it to discrete outlets and away from intervening areas, leaving some high terrace areas that appear to be unglaciated. The outlet glaciers vary in their ice retreat chronology from remaining near their Neoglacial maximum (*e.g.* LaPerouse) to far retracted (*e.g.* Lituya); all have associated deposits extending back into the Pleistocene. Lowlands between the outlets have been carved by the sea into a stepped series of raised terraces, which are surfaced by a complex assortment of marine sedimentary features and glacial deposits of various ages. Some of the oldest terrestrial deposits known in Southeast Alaska are found within the upper terraces.

Significant Sedimentary Records
The uplifted terraces of this province retain perhaps the most important record in Southeast Alaska of events prior to the Last Glacial Maximum. In particular, the sequence of largely unstudied peats atop the high Echo terrace dates to prior to 50,000 ^{14}C yrs BP (Mann, 1983). Ancient moraines (T3) also occupy the terraces; in outlet valleys such as Lituya, Fairweather, Crillon, Dagelet and LaPerouse, huge composite moraines exhibit records where ice and water erosion at their bases have opened them to scrutiny. Mann (1983) has mapped the terrace features, provided a first look at the Echo terrace stratigraphy, and summarized the work of previous researchers, including Goldthwait *et al.* (1963).

Information Sources
As in other provinces, our mapping depended primarily on aerial photo interpretation aided by a history of on-the-ground observations. Mann (1983) has provided a rather detailed map of glacial and outwash features of the terraces, which has provided an additional basis of mapping here.

The Alsek Province

Characterization
Alsek River deposits interfinger with sediments left by the Alsek and other glaciers, whose termini have episodically moved out onto the river's outwash plain. Glaciers within and upstream from the province have occasionally blocked the river in recent centuries, resulting in large outburst floods. The latest of these, in the early 20th century, denuded and reshaped the Dry Bay delta and modified glacial deposits along the valley.

Significant Sedimentary Records
The small valleys and ravines facing north out of the Deception Hills might contain a record of repeated catastrophic floods down the Alsek, but this has not been confirmed by direct observation.

Information Sources
The mapping of this province was based on aerial photography and personal observation.

Conclusions

The first ever surficial geology map that covers all of Glacier Bay National Park and Preserve has been compiled from previously published and unpublished information. The map also covers Gustavus, the islands of Cross Sound / Icy Strait, and the Canadian portion of Glacier Bay's watershed. It is designed to be used at a scale of 1:100,000. Exclusive of areas of snow / ice, water, and no mappable sediments, which cover 84% of the map area, it covers 2475 km^2 with 1364 polygons belonging to 17 surficial sediment units. No attempt was made to map deposits below mean high tide, due to difficulty of observation, and likewise little effort was made to map the deposits of the high mountainous terrain with accuracy.

Literature Cited

Anderson, P. J., R. P. Goldthwait, and G. D. McKenzie. 1986. Observed processes of glacial deposition in Glacier Bay, Alaska: guidebook for INQUA Commission II field conference, 7-16 June 1986, Glacier Bay National Park and Preserve, Alaska. Byrd Polar Research Center, Ohio State University. Columbus, Ohio.

Brew, D., and G. Plafker. *in prep*. Geologic map of Glacier Bay National Park and Preserve. United States Geological Survey.

Capps, D. M., G. C. Wiles, J. J. Clague, and B. H. Luckman. 2011. Tree-ring dating of the nineteenth-century advance of Brady Glacier and the evolution of two ice-marginal lakes, Alaska: The Holocene. v. 21: 641-649.

Connor, C., G. P. Streveler, A. Post, D. Monteith, and W. Howell. 2009. The Neoglacial landscape and human history of Glacier Bay, Glacier Bay National Park and Perserve, southeast Alaska, USA: The Holocene. v. 19: 381-393.

Cooper, W. S. 1937. The problem of Glacier Bay, Alaska: A study of glacier variations: Geographical Review. v. 27: 37-62.

Cowan, E. A., R. D. Powell, and N. D. Smith. 1988. Rainstorm-induced event sedimentation at the tidewater front of a temperate glacier: Geology. v. 16: 409-412.

Cowan, E. A., K. C. Seramur, R. D. Powell, B. A. Willems, S. P. S. Gulick, and J. M. Jaeger. 2010. Fjords as temporary sediment traps; history of glacial erosion and deposition in Muir Inlet, Glacier Bay National Park, Southeastern Alaska: Geological Society of America Bulletin. v. 122: 1067-1080.

Derkson, S. J. 1976. Glacial geology of the Brady Glacier region, Alaska. The Ohio State University, Institute of Polar Studies. Columbus, Ohio.

Farr, T. G., P. A. Rosen, E. Caro, R. Crippen, R. Duren, S. Hensley, M. Kobrick, M. Paller, E. Rodriguez, L. Roth, D. Seal, S. Shaffer, J. Shimada, J. Umland, M. Werner, M. Oskin, D. Burbank, and D. Alsdork. 2007. The Shuttle Radar Topography Mission: Reviews of Geophysics. v. 45: RG2004.

Gehrels, G. E., and H. C. Berg. 1992. Geologic map of southeastern Alaska, Map I-1867. Miscellaneous Investigations Series. United States Geological Survey.

Goldthwait, R. P. 1961. Dating the Little Ice Age in Glacier Bay, Alaska. International Geological Congress XXI. Norden.

Goldthwait, R. P. 1966. Glacial history. 18. Mirsky, A. editor. Soil development and ecological succession in a deglaciated area of Muir Inlet, southeastern Alaska. The Ohio State University, Institute of Polar Studies. Columbus, Ohio.

Goldthwait, R. P. 1986. Glacial history of Glacier Bay Park area. Anderson, P. J., R. P. Goldthwait, and G. D. McKenzie. editors. Observed processes of glacial deposition in Glacier Bay, Alaska. The Ohio State University, Miscellaneous Publication of the Byrd Polar Research Center volume 236. Columbus, Ohio. Pages 5-16.

Goldthwait, R. P., I. C. McKellar, and C. Cronk. 1963. Fluctuations of Crillon Glacier, southeast Alaska: International Association of Scientific Hydrologists Bulletin. v. 8: 62-74.

Goodwin, R. G. 1984. Neoglacial lacustrine sedimentation and ice advance, Glacier Bay, Alaska. Institute of Polar Studies Report 79. The Ohio State University. Columbus, Ohio. 183 pages.

Haselton, G. M. 1966. Glacial geology of Muir Inlet, Alaska. The Ohio State University, Institute of Polar Studies. Columbus, Ohio.

Haselton, G. M. 1984. Glacial geology of Tarr Inlet and vicinity, Glacier Bay National Monument, Alaska, 1975. Oehser, P. H., J. S. Lea, and N. L. Pomars, eds. Research Reports. 16. National Geographic Society. Washington, D.C.

Larsen, C. F., R. J. Motyka, J. T. Freymueller, K. A. Echelmeyer, and E. r. Ivins. 2004. Rapid uplift of southern Alaska caused by recent ice loss: Geophysical Journal International. v. 158: 1118-1133.

Larson, G. J. 1978. Meltwater storage in a temperate glacier, Burroughs Glacier, Southeast Alaska. Institute of Polar Studies. Columbus, Ohio.

Lawson, D. 2011. Personal communication, E-mail to Greg Streveler.

Lawson, D. *ca*. 2009. Stratigraphic chart from near Reid Glacier with associated dates. E-mail communication to Greg Streveler.

MacKevett, E. M., D. A. Brew, C. C. Hawley, L. C. Huff, and F. G. Smith. 1971. Mineral Resources of Glacier Bay National Monument, Alaska: USGS Professional Paper. v. 632: 90 pages + maps.

Mann, D. H. 1983. The Quaternary history of the Lituya glacial refugium, Alaska. Ph.D. Dissertation, University of Washington. Seattle.

Mann, D. H., and G. P. Streveler. 2008. Post-glacial relative sea level, isostasy, and glacial history in Icy Strait, Southeast Alaska, USA: Quaternary Research. v. 69: 201-216.

McKenzie, G. D. 1970. Glacial geology of Adams Inlet, southeastern Alaska. Institute of Polar Studies Report 25. The Ohio State University. Columbus, Ohio.

McKenzie, G. D. 1986. Ice-contact and deltaic processes and deposits, Adams Inlet. 99-121. Anderson, P. J., R. P. Goldthwait, and G. D. McKenzie. editors. Observed processes of glacial deposition in Glacier Bay, Alaska. The Ohio State University, Institue of Polar Studies. Columbus, Ohio.

MDA Federal. 2004. Landsat GeoCover 2000/ETM+ Edition Mosaics, Tile N-08-55_2000. NASA, ed. USGS. Souix Falls, South Dakota.

Mickelson, D. M. 1971. Glacial geology of the Burroughs Glacier area, southeastern Alaska. The Ohio State University. Columbus, OH.

Motyka, R. J., C. F. Larsen, J. T. Freymueller, and K. A. Echelmeyer. 2007. Post Little Ice Age glacial rebound in Glacier Bay National Park and surrounding areas: Alaska Park Science. v. 6: 36-41.

Peterson, D. N., and G. D. McKenzie. 1968. Observations of a glacier cave in Glacier Bay National Monument, Alaska: The National Speleological Society Bulletin. v. 30: 47-54.

Powell, R. D. 1983. Glacial-marine sedimentation processes and lithofacies of temperate tidewater glaciers, Glacier Bay, Alaska. 844. Molnia, B. F. editor. Glacial-Marine Sedimentation. Plenum Press. New York.

Powell, R. D., and P. R. Carlson. 1997. Evaluation of conditions along the grounding line of temperate marine glaciers: an example from Muir Inlet, Glacier Bay, Alaska: Marine Geology. v. 140: 307-327.

Price, R. J. 1964. Landforms produced by the wastage of the Casement Glacier, southeast Alaska. The Ohio State University, Institute of Polar Studies. Columbus, Ohio.

Raup, B., and Siri Jodha S. Khalsa. 2010. GLIMS Analysis Tutorial. 2012. http://glims.org/MapsAndDocs/assets/GLIMS_Analysis_Tutorial_letter.pdf

Rossman, D. L. 1958. Geology and ore deposits in the Reid Inlet area Glacier Bay, Alaska: With notes on a mineralized area near Lituya Bay, Geological Survey Bulletin 1058-B. United States Government Printing Office. Washington.

Seramur, K. C., R. D. Powell, and P. R. Carlson. 1997. Evaluation of conditions along the grounding line of temperate marine glaciers; an example from Muir Inlet, Glacier Bay, Alaska: Marine Geology. v. 140: 307-327.

Syverson, K. M. 1992. Glacial geology of the southeastern Burroughs Glacier, Glacier Bay National Park and Preserve, Alaska.University of Wisconsin. Madison.

Taylor, L. D. 1962. Ice structures, Burroughs Glacier, southeast Alaska. Ph.D. Thesis. The Ohio State University. Columbus, OH.

Trusel, L. D., G. R. Cochrane, L. L. Etherington, R. D. Powell, and L. A. Mayer. 2010. Marine benthic habitat mapping of Muir Inlet, Glacier Bay National Park and Preserve, Alaska, with an evaluation of the Coastal and Marine Ecological Classification Standard III. U.S. Geological Survey Scientific Investigations Map 3122.

Wiles, G. C., D. E. Lawson, E. Lyon, N. Wiesenberg, and R. D. D'Arrigo. 2011. Tree-ring dates on two pre-Little Ice Age advances in Glacier Bay National Park and Preserve, Alaska, USA: Quaternary Research. v. 76: 190-195.

Appendix A: Glossary

^{14}C age – the length of time since the death of an organism based on the radioactive decay of an isotope of carbon in its body. Due to historical and scientific reasons, radiocarbon years are not quite the equivalent of calendar years, and hence we specify in the report whether we are referring to ^{14}C or calendar years.

Algorithm – a set of rules for solving a problem in a finite number of steps (e.g., a computer program).

Alluvial Fan – a fan-shaped deposit in map view, typically composed of sand and gravel, deposited by a stream. See figures B1 and B3 in the photo appendix.

ArcGIS – the mapping software, made by ESRI, which was used in this mapping project. We used version 9.2.

Beach Ridges – a continuous mound of beach material (typically sand) behind the beach that was heaped up by waves or wind action.

BP – an abbreviation for "Before Present," which, by convention, is considered to be 1950.

Collapse Features – hummocky or uneven surfaces resulting from the melting of ice buried by sediment. See figures B7, B8, B10, and B13 in the photo appendix.

Delta – the equivalent of an alluvial fan that is built into a water body.

Dendrochronology – the method of dating events by counting and correlating tree rings.

Deposits – material that has accumulated by a natural process.

DOQQ – a Digital Orthophoto Quarter Quadrangle; a vertical aerial photograph covering 3½ minutes of longitude by 3½ minutes of latitude that has been modified to remove distortions, enabling the DOQQ to be used like a map.

Esker – a ridge generally composed of sand and gravel deposited by a stream in a tunnel beneath a glacier. See figures B9 and B11 in the photo appendix.

ESRI – Environmental Systems Research Institute, Inc.; a company that produces software for the creation of maps and the analysis of geographic data, specifically, it produces the mapping software that we used for this project, ArcGIS 9.2.

Geomorphologist – a scientist of landscapes.

Glaciolacustrine – related to the interaction of glacial and lake processes.

Glaciomarine – related to the interaction of glacial and marine processes.

Holocene – the last 10,000 ^{14}C years of Earth history.

Ice-Contact Sediment – sediment (sand, gravel, boulders, *etc.*) that was deposited on, under, or immediately adjacent to a glacier.

Isostatic Rebound – the process by which the Earth's surface rises in elevation as a response to the removal of the weight of glacial ice.

Kame – ice-contact sediment, generally sand and gravel, deposited in a more or less conical hill.

Loess – an accumulation of silt-sized particles that was transported and deposited by the wind.

Neoglacial – a period of cooler temperatures beginning about 5,000 ^{14}C yrs BP.

Oblique Aerial Photo – a photograph taken from a plane or helicopter where the camera was pointing at some angle other than directly downward, in contrast to a vertical aerial photograph.

Outwash – sand, or sand and gravel, deposited by streams flowing away from a glacier. See figure B4 in the photo appendix.

Outwash Plain - a flat area created by the deposition of outwash. See figures B2 and B3 in the photo appendix.

Pleistocene – the time span that encompasses the most recent major ice ages between about 2.6 million calendar and 10,000 ^{14}C years ago.

Radiocarbon – see ^{14}C age.

Sediment – clay to boulder-sized grains deposited by water, wind, ice, or gravity.

Silt – particles between 0.625 mm and 0.002 mm in diameter (smaller than sand; larger than clay).

SRTM – Shuttle Radar Topography Mission

Stratigraphy – a collection of discrete sedimentary layers, such as those comprising our map units.

Topset beds – the nearly horizontal layers of sediment deposited by streams on top of a growing delta.

Vertical Aerial Photo – a photograph taken from a plane or helicopter where the camera was orientated straight toward the ground, in contrast to an oblique aerial photograph.

Appendix B: Photo Companion

Our goal for this section is to aid novice geomorphologists in gaining a practical sense of what our map units represent. With that in mind, we have selected the photographs that best illustrate the map area's sediments. Modern examples are shown more frequently than Holocene and Pleistocene surfaces because the older features are generally too vegetated for easy viewing of the underlying landforms. The photographs are all either oblique views from low-level flight or views from the ground and all of them are more detailed than the map. As a result, we have refrained from identifying the photo locations because they generally depict features that are too small to show on the map. As a reminder, the map was constructed from vertical aerial photographs, the published literature, and observations by the authors over previous years. Because of the greater detail in these photos, they should serve as useful illustrations for what the map units look like in the field.

Figure B1: Low-level oblique aerial photograph of an alluvial fan mapped as modern stream sediment (S1). Colluvium (abbreviated as "C" on the map) surrounds the fan on two sides and water is on the third side. The letter "N" indicates deposits not thick enough to map.

Figure B2: Low-level oblique aerial photograph of braided stream surface mapped as S1 (modern stream sediment). The surface in the background is older till (T2). I1 is a collapsing ice-contact sediment complex that is less than 100 calendar years old.

Figure B3: Low-level oblique aerial photograph of braided stream surface mapped as S1 (modern stream sediment) and colluvium (C) as indicated. Higher areas have sediment too thin to map (N).

Figure B4: Vertical face showing thin till over Holocene sand and gravel (T/S2) near Wachusett Inlet.

Figure B5: Freshly exposed till surface (T1) near the Burroughs Glacier.

Figure B6: Recently deposited till (T1) being exposed by a retreating glacier edge (upper left). The shovel handle is about 20 inches long.

Figure B7: Ground-based photo of debris-covered ice (I1-- ice contact sediment complex). Note the circled people for scale.

Figure B8: Low-level oblique aerial photograph of debris-covered ice that is actively melting (modern ice-contact sediment complex—I1). Clean glacier ice was mapped as "snow / ice". Upland has deposits too thin to map (N).

Figure B9: Close-up of esker being exposed by the melting of overlying ice. Without ice cover this would be mapped as a modern ice-contact sediment complex (I1).

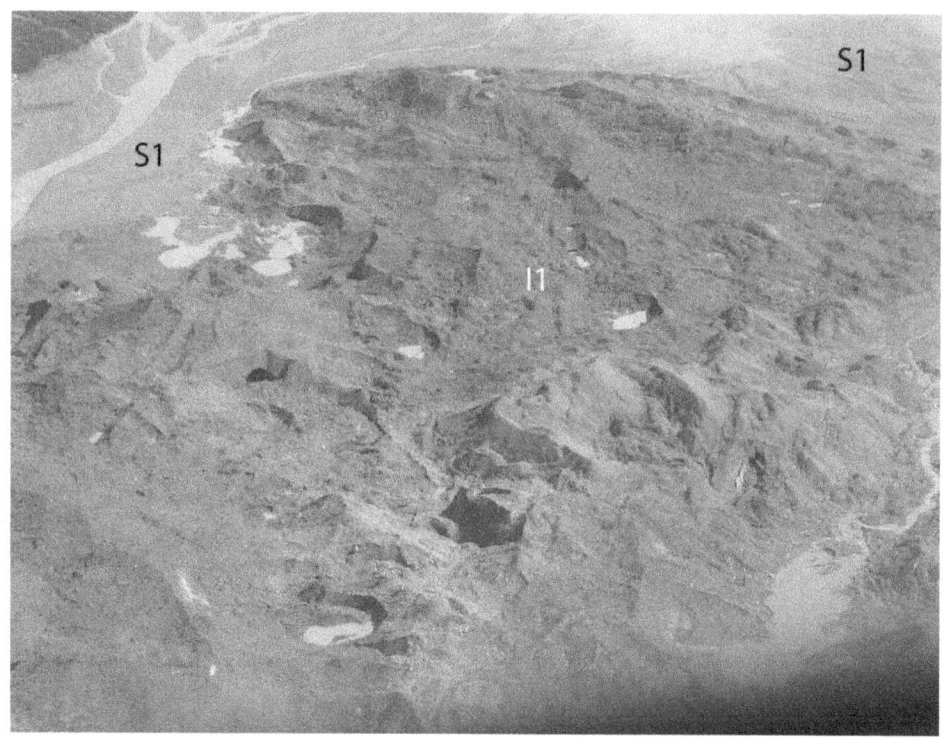

Figure B10: Low-level oblique aerial photograph of hummocky supraglacial debris mapped as a modern ice-contact sediment complex (I1) and as a modern braided stream surface (S1).

Figure B11: Close-up of a small esker and surrounding collapsing sand and gravel (modern ice-contact sediment complex – I1). Also shown is colluvium (C) and areas were deposits are too thin to map (N).

Figure B12: Low-level oblique aerial photograph of an area in front of a glacier showing modern braided stream surface (S1), collapsing sand and gravel (modern ice-contact sediment complex – I1), and a freshly exposed till surface (T1). Deposits on upland are too thin to map (N).

Figure B13: Low-level oblique aerial photograph showing recently exposed till surface (T1) and collapsing sand and gravel (modern ice contact sediment complex – I1). The glacier ice has a very thin debris cover and so is mapped as "snow / ice."

Figure B14: Ground photo of a modern lake-sediment complex (L1) and recent till (T1). The lake sediment on the far side overlay's sand, gravel, and till.

Figure B15: Ground photo of a modern lake sediment complex (L1) and recent till (T1). Shovel handle is about 20 inches long. Lake sediment is sand and indicates at least two lake levels.

Figure B16: Close-up photo of sand- and silt-sized particles typical of lake sediment complexes. This example is from a modern one (L1) but Holocene (L2) and Pleistocene (L3) examples would be similar.

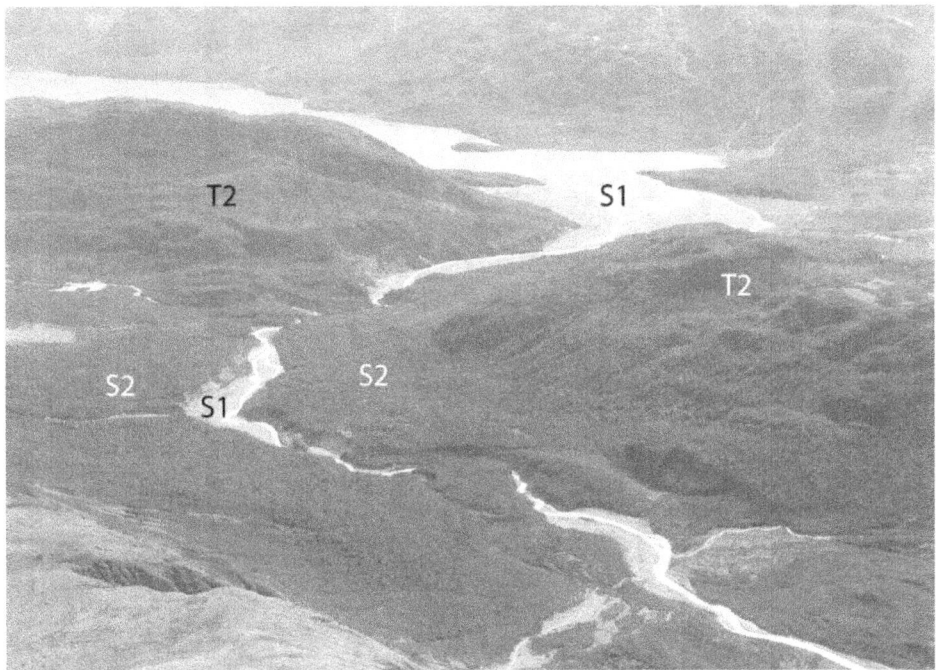

Figure B17: Low-level oblique photo of a fully vegetated outwash plain (S2) and modern braided stream sediment (S1). Uplands are covered with thin till (T2).

Figure B18: Low-level oblique photo of fully vegetated uplands with thin till (T2) and a fully vegetated and stabilized ice-contact sediment complex (I2). A small area of modern stream sediment is also visible (S1).

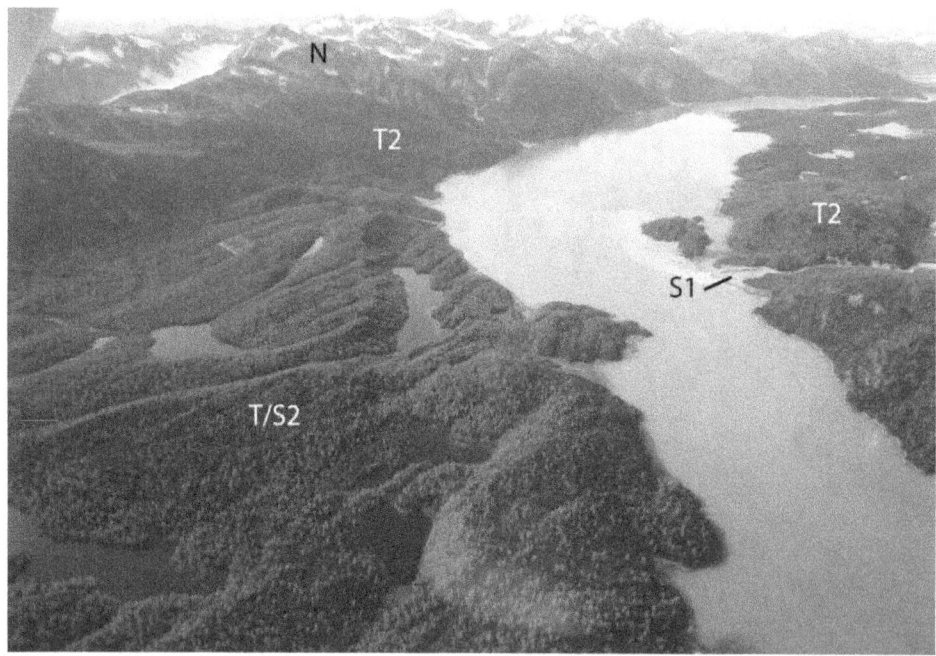

Figure B19: Low-level oblique photo showing modern stream sediment (S1) (alluvial fan). Areas shown as T2 are fully vegetated till surfaces with bedrock beneath and the area shown as T/S2 has thin till over Holocene sand and gravel. The letter N indicates uplands where deposits are too thin to map.

Figure B20: Close-up of tree stump buried in Holocene sand and gravel that is widespread in Muir Inlet and is typically covered by till. This is mapped as T/S2.

Figure B21: Low-level oblique photo of a late Neoglacial outwash plain (stream sediment – S2). In this area the outwash is reworked into a marine sediment complex (M2). The modern beach can be seen in the distance (M1).

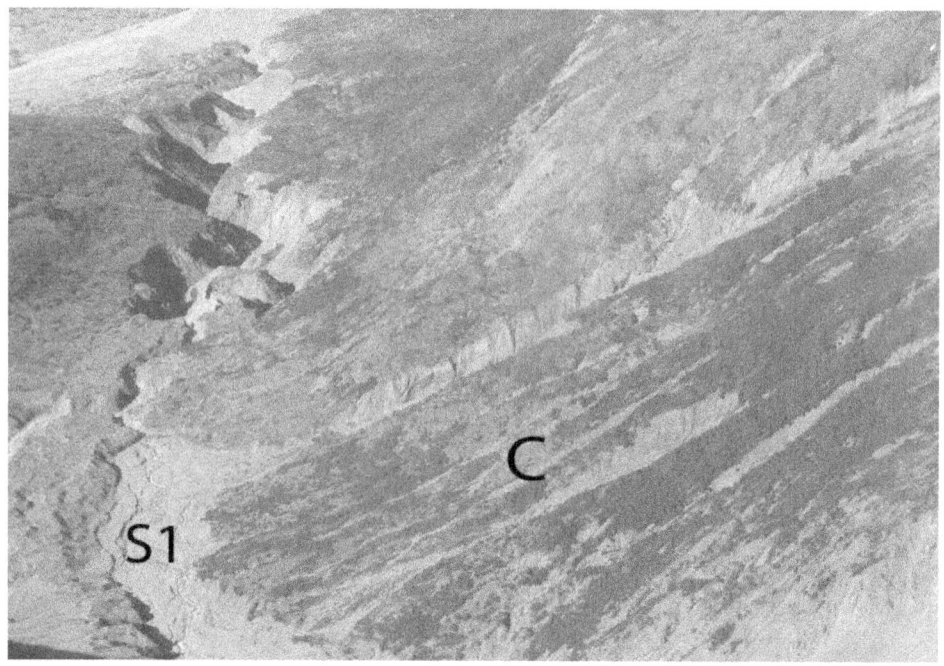

Figure B22: Low-level oblique photo showing colluvium (C) at base of the slope and modern stream sediment along the bottom (S1).

Figure B23: Low-level oblique photo showing uplands that were not mapped in this study.

Figure B24: Low-level oblique photo showing uplands that were not mapped in this study.

Figure B25: An outcrop exposure of Pleistocene till (T3).

43

Figure B26: An outcrop of Pleistocene marine sediment (M3). In this particular example the sediment is sand and gravel and the layers are dipping to the right; this was once a delta that was building out into the sea. The dipping layers were deposited below sea level, thus we characterize it as marine sediment. If, however, the sediment had been deposited a few hundred meters upstream of this location, it would have been above sea level at the time of its deposition and we would have classified it as Pleistocene stream sediment (S3). Because marine sediments can also include the clays and silts that are deposited in quieter waters, as well as the sands, gravels, and boulders of higher energy environments such as beaches, we call this assortment of sediments a "marine sediment complex" to emphasize the variety of particle sizes that are included within this category.

Appendix C: Algorithm for Mapping Snow / Ice from LandSat Mosaics

For the purposes of more fully documenting our methods and potentially assisting others with the automated mapping of glacier extents we include the following step-by-step directions for how we performed the procedure using ArcGIS 9.2. A word of caution, the detailed instructions below might not translate well to other mapping programs or even newer versions of ArcGIS, although the underlying principle of selecting pixels by their color and then filtering the resulting selections by size would remain valid. Also, there are online resources to assist with this task that we were not aware of at the time (e.g., Raup and Khalsa, 2010).

Here are the steps that we employed:

1- Zoom to the area of interest.
2- Bring up the spatial analyst toolbar.
3- Under the spatial analyst's options change the extent to visible extent.
4- LandSat mosaics are composed of three bands; by assigning Band 1 the color red, Band 2 green, and Band 3 blue a reasonable approximation of true colors can be made. Use the raster calculator to select the pixels that have a Band 1 value <50, a Band 2 value >100, and a Band 3 value >102. This will select the white and light blue areas of the mosaic.
5- The raster calculator will create a new map layer where all pixels have been assigned a 1 or a 0 depending on whether or not the pixel meets the above criteria. At first pass it will likely appear that the glaciers have all been selected appropriately, but closer examination will reveal that the portions of glaciers covered by debris, thin clouds, or shadows were *not* selected and that some isolated bits of the shoreline *were* selected.
6- Remove the non-glacier areas from view and change the glacier areas to a highly visible color for easy viewing.
7- To filter out the isolated shoreline selections, do a 10 x 10 grid selection (which is under Neighborhood Statistics) that will calculate the ratio of selected cells to non-selected within a 10x10 box centered on the pixel of interest.
8- Then reclassify all cells with a mean value greater than 0.3 and convert these selections to polygon format. These areas, with some additional manual editing, will become the glaciers.
9- Digitize the additional glacier areas that are covered by debris, clouds, or shadows and the job is done.

Appendix D: Autobiographies of the Authors

We have chosen to provide a few words about our backgrounds because so often in this text we have called upon our experiences in this landscape to explain our mapping choices. In making the map we first digitized previously existing surficial geology maps, which collectively covered ~3% of the map area, and then we used aerial photography to interpret the remainder, but it was not so much that we examined aerial photography, as it was that we examined aerial photography through the lens of our experiences in this landscape. While there are many places in the map area that we have not been to, there are also many places that we have seen in the field. So, it is not so much that the map is not based on field work, as it is that the map is based on time spent in the field over many years. We hope that you, the reader, have been, or will be, as fortunate. In the near immortal words of Aldo Leopold, "*I am glad I shall never be young without wild country to be young in.*"

Richard Becker – Richard Becker earned a B.S. in Geological Sciences from the University of Maine in 2003, writing an Honors Thesis on some of the glaciomarine sediments of the state. The project was his first introduction to Glacier Bay, for many of the seminal works on analogous modern features were conducted in Muir Inlet. He continued his glacial geology education at the University of Wisconsin-Madison, graduating with a M.S. degree in 2005, and spent the following four summers (2006-2009) working as an Interpretive Park Ranger in Glacier Bay National Park and Preserve.

Gregory Streveler – Greg Streveler earned a B.S. and M.S. in ecology and geology at the University of Wisconsin-Madison in the 1960s. He worked as a ranger and then research scientist at Glacier Bay National Park prior to 1980, during which time he facilitated and contributed to a variety of geologic studies, notably those associated with the Institute of Polar Studies and U.S. Geological Survey. As a private contractor since then, he has maintained a professional presence in the park. In recent decades his research has centered on sediments associated with former sea levels along the park's southern periphery, and on the recent geological history of lower Glacier Bay.

David Mickelson – Dave Mickelson earned an A.B. in Geography from Clark University in 1966, a M.S. in Geology from the University of Maine in 1968, and a Ph.D. in Geology from the Institute of Polar Studies at The Ohio State University in 1971. For his dissertation research he investigated the glacial geology and modern processes of the Burroughs and Plateau Glaciers near Muir Inlet. While teaching in the Department of Geology and Geophysics at the University of Wisconsin-Madison between 1971 and 2005, he and his graduate students did research in Glacier Bay every decade from the 1970s through the 1990s. He has also mapped and interpreted glacial deposits in many other areas of the world.

The Department of the Interior protects and manages the nation's natural resources and cultural heritage; provides scientific and other information about those resources; and honors its special responsibilities to American Indians, Alaska Natives, and affiliated Island Communities.

NPS 1321/117432, October 2012